AMERICA'S FAVORITE SYMBOLS

THE LIBERTY BELL

RINGING IN AMERICA'S INDEPENDENCE

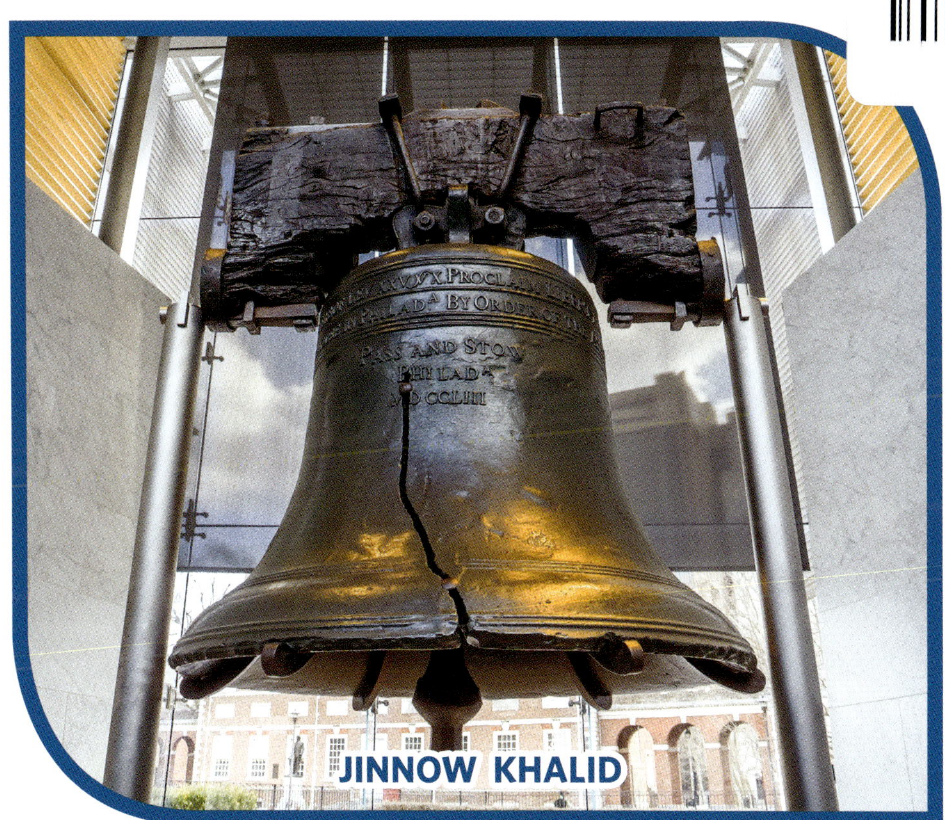

JINNOW KHALID

New York

Published in 2021 by The Rosen Publishing Group, Inc.
29 East 21st Street, New York, NY 10010

First Edition

Portions of this work were originally authored by Maria Nelson and published as *The Liberty Bell*. All new material in this edition was authored by Jinnow Khalid.

Editor: Elizabeth Krajnik
Book Design: Reann Nye

Photo Credits: Cover, pp.1, 5 f11photo/Shutterstock.com; Series Art sunwart/Shutterstock.com; p. 7 Photographs in the Carol M. Highsmith Archive, Library of Congress, Prints and Photographs Division; p. 9 Three Lions/Hulton Archive/Getty Images; p. 11 From a painting by Leah Anderson Joseph copyright © 2002 Liberty Bell Shrine, Inc. All rights reserved.; p. 13 Courtesy of the Library of Congress; p. 15 Archive Photos/Getty Images; p. 17 Hulton Archive/Archive Photos/Getty Images; p. 19 Buyenlarge/Archive Photos/Getty Images; p. 21 The World in HDR/Shutterstock.com; p. 22 Edwin Verin/Shutterstock.com.

Library of Congress Cataloging-in-Publication Data

Names: Khalid, Jinnow, author.
Title: The Liberty Bell : Ringing in America's Independence / Jinnow Khalid.
Description: New York : PowerKids Press, 2020. | Series: America's favorite symbols | Includes index.
Identifiers: LCCN 2019045549 | ISBN 9781725317222 (paperback) | ISBN 9781725317246 (library binding) | ISBN 9781725317239 (6 pack) | ISBN 9781725317253 (ebook)
Subjects: LCSH: Liberty Bell–Juvenile literature. | Philadelphia (Pa.)–Buildings, structures, etc.–Juvenile literature.
Classification: LCC F158.8.I3 K43 2020 | DDC 974.8/11–dc23
LC record available at https://lccn.loc.gov/2019045549

Manufactured in the United States of America

CPSIA Compliance Information: Batch #CSPK20. For Further Information contact Rosen Publishing, New York, New York at 1-800-237-9932.

CONTENTS

Seeing Liberty

You've probably heard the word "liberty." Liberty is the state of being able to act and speak freely. But you can't see liberty itself. Throughout the history of the United States, people have known the Liberty Bell as a **symbol** of liberty.

PASS AND STOW
PHILADA
MDCCLIII

Ordering the Bell

In 1751, the Pennsylvania government ordered a bell to **celebrate** 50 years of Pennsylvania's original **constitution**. It would hang in the State House (now **Independence** Hall) in Philadelphia, Pennsylvania. The bell cracked when it was tested in 1752.

PHILADA BY ORDER
PASS AND STOW
PHILADA
MDCCLIII

Recasting the Bell

The Liberty Bell was originally known as the State House bell. Philadelphia metalworkers melted the cracked bell down to make another bell. This bell rang to call lawmakers to important meetings and to call the townspeople to hear the news.

PROCLAIM LIBERTY
BY ORDER OF THE
PASS AND STOW
PHILAD^A
MDCCLIII

Hiding the Bell

In 1777, during the **American Revolution**, patriots removed the bell from the State House and took it to Allentown, Pennsylvania. They hid it in a church because they were afraid the British soldiers would melt it down to make cannons.

Liberty for All

In 1778, American soldiers returned the bell to the State House. In the 1800s, an antislavery **publication** first gave the State House bell the name "Liberty Bell." However, this name didn't catch on until years later. In 1847, a story used the Liberty Bell to symbolize national pride.

TO GOD IN
1876.

Another Crack

In 1835, the Liberty Bell cracked while ringing for Chief Justice John Marshall's **funeral**. Metalworkers fixed it, but the work wasn't completely successful. The bell cracked more when it rang in February 1846 for George Washington's birthday. It hasn't rung since.

PASS & STOW
PHILADA
MDCCLIII

Road Trip!

From 1885 to 1915, the Liberty Bell traveled throughout the United States by train. It stopped in New Orleans, Chicago, Atlanta, Charleston, Boston, Saint Louis, and San Francisco. The Liberty Bell reminded people of how they worked together for independence.

ROCLAIM
584

Replica Bells

In 1915, Pennsylvania suffragists, or people fighting for women's right to vote, had a **replica** Liberty Bell made. It was called the Justice Bell. Today, you can visit 57 full-size Liberty Bell replicas throughout the world. There's even one at Walt Disney World!

ESTABLISH JUSTICE
THEREOF ✶ PROCLAIM
TROY, N.Y.

Visit the Bell

In 1976, the Liberty Bell was moved from Independence Hall. Today, you can visit the bell inside the Liberty Bell Center, which is nearby. About 2 million people visit the Liberty Bell each year.

PROCLAIM
PHILADA BY ORDER OF THE
PASS AND STOW
PHILADA
MDCCLIII

Parts of the Liberty Bell

GLOSSARY

American Revolution: The war of 1775–1783 in which 13 British colonies in North America broke free from British rule and became the United States of America.

celebrate: To do something special or enjoyable for an important event or holiday.

constitution: A document that describes the system of beliefs and laws by which a country, state, or organization is governed.

funeral: A ceremony held for a dead person.

independence: Freedom from outside control or support.

publication: A book, magazine, etc., that has been printed and made available to the public.

replica: An exact copy of something.

symbol: Something that stands for something else.

INDEX

WEBSITES

Due to the changing nature of Internet links, PowerKids Press has developed an online list of websites related to the subject of this book. This site is updated regularly. Please use this link to access the list: www.powerkidslinks.com/afs/libertybell